INDEPENDENT MINDSET

Developing your self-standing thought

By

LARRY ASH

ISBN: 9798846515468

CONTENTS

Introduction

Being independent minded doesn't necessarily mean that your opinions are always different from others and that you never consult with other people; it means simply that you hold opinions because they make sense to you.

Individuals who are independent minded aren't afraid of having a different opinion but don't simply pick an opposing view just to be different.

An independent life provides you with self-reliance, happiness, confidence, and security and you are able to manage yourself in a complex world at larg.

This book has a wealth of information that can aid in cultivating an independent thinking.

There are many points put together in this book that can be of help to develop independent mindset

CHAPTER 1:
The concepts of independent mindset

Independent

The ability to take care of oneself, and make decisions on their own, without the influence of any other person. Undertaking all the responsibilities and tasks on your own. Having the ability to find happiness within oneself.

The key thing to note is that being independent does not mean competing with other people's opinions. It entails being aware of your strengths and weaknesses and having the strength to overcome challenges on your own.

A person becomes independent in their thinking and their actions. Being independent is learning to stand on your own and being accepting of your circumstances. If all else fails, you can take care of yourself and others.

Mindset

Mindset speaks to a person's attitude or mental state. It is a person's self-concept that reinforces beliefs, attitudes, and feelings of oneself. It is our innate self-dialogue. These dialogues are created from our experiences, beliefs, cultures, and attitudes. Our thoughts, beliefs, and actions create rippling effects in our lives and produce new information to process.

Our mindset promotes growth or stagnation, depending on our experiences and self-dialogue. We should grow with each experience that crosses our path. Rid ourselves of limiting beliefs and be willing to improve our lives.

The Benefits of an Independent Life

1. **It increases your sense of worth and self-assurance.**
A rise in self-esteem results in a good attitude on oneself, and an increase in self-confidence indicates that you trust yourself to be competent in the conditions you face. Learning independence gives you confidence since you know you have the skills and abilities to overcome any obstacle.

2. **It lessens the strain you put on your loved ones, friends, and society.** You don't need to rely on other people for assistance if you can use technology to meet your own requirements. You lessen others' burdens rather than adding to them.

3. **It makes you more valuable as a resource for others.** It's okay to require assistance. Everyone will

eventually require it. However, independence also brings with it the capacity to take care of oneself and assist others as needed. People come to rely on you as a valuable resource and turn to you for support.

4. **It enhances your reputation among friends and colleagues.**
People perceive you favorably as a contributor to society rather than a dependent when you demonstrate your independence. How far you may advance in life today is determined on your reputation. Being independent builds a strong reputation.

5. **It leads to financial freedom because you are skilled and capable.** You have the ability to work and generate money so that you may take care of yourself and plan for the future. Independence is empowering, but financial instability is frightening.

6. **It gives you social skill and dexterity.**
The world in which we live is social, both offline and online through interactions on social media. Being independent gives you the freedom to move around society and interact with people, which is a

quality that is necessary for creature a social being. This makes it possible for collaboration, networking, and friendship.

7. **It gives you the physical capacity to look after both other people and yourself.** Regardless of any physical limitations, the more physically capable you become, the better you will be able to handle situations in your environment.

8. **It fills you with a sense of joy and happiness that can come from no other source.** Independence, self-worth, the capacity to interact with and assist others, and physical activity all contribute to happiness.

9. You become mobile as opposed to being limited to your neighborhood. This entails that you have the freedom to behave, move, and work as you like. You are not constrained by your existing situation and have the power to improve it.

10. It positions you for future growth and independence. Because you can depend on yourself, you can stay up with technology, and with that resource, you can achieve everything you set your mind to and have the capacity for endless advancement. You are able to keep ahead of the changes and make the necessary adjustments rather than falling behind with each new technological advancement.

VISION

We are visual animals when it comes to survival. Our eyesight is the most advanced sense we have as a species. Our stereoscopic vision can distinguish a wide range of hues and tones. This thus makes it simple for us to see patterns and motion. We were able to escape becoming meal while attempting to procure our own dinner thanks to our combined skills. We succeeded physically because of our vision, and we still do.

Vision is crucial to survival when it comes to life

success. This vision, however, uses our feeling of possibility and imagination rather than our sense of sight. The ability to envision successful outcomes is what is meant by vision in the context of life. It is the capacity to envision fruitful outcomes. At its core, it is the capacity to dream clearly about the direction you want to take your life.

Do not hesitate to dream. According to Henry Ford, whether you believe you can do a task or believe you cannot, you are correct. Therefore, take a few minutes each day to visualize your destination and the route you will take to get there. By no means is this daydreaming. This is organized, scheduled, and development-focused. Consider the best possible results as you plan your day. Athletes adopt the same technique to improve their performance. You are more likely to achieve success if you picture yourself achieving. Always keep in mind that if you don't take the time to construct your own ambitions, someone else will hire you to build theirs.

FOCUS

Usually, when we speak of focus, we're referring to physical activity. Yet, focus is as important in our independent life. In life, endurance usually takes the form of focus. Instead of physical prowess, it becomes the ability to concentrate successfully on a given task.
Focus is a critical skill to build independent thought, especially in today's fast paced world where success often means keeping several equally important balls in the air at one time.

So, how do you focus on multitasking, a situation where, by its very definition, several things are happening at once? Well, the key to successful focus is attention. When several things are happening simultaneously, you need to concentrate on only one thing at a time. This doesn't mean that you bring one task to full completion before you start on another. Rather, you spend just enough time on a given task to take it to the next stage of development and then you turn your attention to another task. In some sense, it's a little like being a mother duck with ducklings. You give your attention to the duckling that is farthest out of line, nudging it forward to where it should be before you turn your attention to the next little duck. Each duckling gets a measure of your focus, but none gets your full attention all the time. In this way, every of your task gets moved along in turn, and all are successfully completed in time.

Take risk

There are people who are natural risk takers, as well as people who are very risk adverse. The key to independent when it comes to risk-taking is understanding what type of person you are and how this personality trait can affect your life when it comes to dealing with risk. It is important to keep in mind that the secret of success when it comes to risk is mitigating potential damage in favor of potential gain. Therefore, neither type of risk personality, in and of itself, provides an advantage over the other when it comes to risk management. A risk taker can just as easily over reach themselves as a risk adverse person can under reach themselves.

When faced with a situation that offers reward and risk, the key is to coolly and impartially assess the potential positive and negative outcomes and decide accordingly. Independent minded people are sometimes seen as risk-takers simply because they understand the danger in a situation better than anyone else involved. So, while it appears that they are courting disaster, the reality is that the risks involved have been managed so as to control negative consequences.

Take Responsibility

This one is fairly straightforward. President Harry Truman had a sign on his desk that said: "The buck stops here". What he meant by that was, as President, he did not have the option to pass the buck when it came to mistakes or failure. He was the boss and the buck stopped getting passed with him.

That's pretty smart advice for any body who wants to be more independent. When it comes to the results of the decisions you make, don't pass the buck. Everyone is happy to take credit for a positive outcome; as well they should if they were directly responsible for that outcome. That's the easy part. The hard part is owning up to your own mistakes.

There is somewhat of an inclination to try and blame someone or something else for a negative outcome. The most successful people fight that inclination and accept the

blame for their mistakes as readily as they accept

congratulations for their successes. They do so because they realize that being the captain of the ship means that all decisions start and end with you. If you happen to make a bad decision then you own that fact, tighten your belt and move forward armed with the knowledge on how never to repeat that mistake. This is a part of the process of independent mindset. It is a process that demonstrates that the greatest opportunity arises from failure. By avoiding the repercussions of that failure, you also avoid the opportunity to grow as a person and learn from your own mistakes. In other words, you condemn yourself to make that same mistake over and over. So, if and when you are faced with a bad life situation of your own making, don't pass the buck. The buck stops with you. Accept that and move on.

Mindfulness

Experience is a great teacher. Each day, all of our lives are jam-packed with numerous experiences. A lot of these experiences are everyday occurrences. Others are less common. Occasionally, some are so unique that they are literally life-changing. However, whether the experience is mundane or out of this world, it offers us a teaching moment. Most of us will, hopefully, come away from a unique experience with a fresh perspective. Yet, very few of us grasp the enlightenment that is inherent in the day-to-day activities that, by necessity, take up the majority of our time. Buddhists call this awareness of the learning potential in the commonplace “mindfulness”. Independent minded people understand this concept and utilize it to their advantage.

When you begin to be mindful, you see that everything that you do has merit. You also realize that no matter what you are doing, you are capable of doing it better. In life, this means that you begin to pay closer attention to every task.

You understand that each task fits into others and together they comprise the whole of your life. If you take a shortcut or cut corners on the smallest of things it only serves to undermine the largest and seemingly most important jobs. Likewise, when you attempt to do the most basic of jobs to the very best of your ability this mindful mindset carries over into other areas and brings a new level of excellence to your entire enterprise. So, use every experience, every day, as a moment to learn.

Be mindful of bad or lazy behaviors and work to change them into more positive and productive actions. Your entire life will benefit from this simple attention to detail.

Be Competitive

The world is built, to some extent, on the concept of competition. Everything living competes for specific resources that are needed to grow, thrive and outperform ecological rivals. Sunlight, space, water, and nutrients are utilized to the fullest extent by the smallest to largest creatures wherever they are found and in whatever quantities. As human beings, we are hardwired to engage in this competitive contest too. It’s a part of our genetic heritage and one every business owner needs to embrace.

The problem is that some people perceive competition as a somewhat undesirable trait. This is because these people look at competition as a black and white issue. It is seen as either a win at all cost, take no prisoners proposition or as a watered down and barely discernible version of itself, where consensus and agreement are the order of the day. This imposed polarity masks the true nature and power of competition. In reality, competitiveness is neither a black or white extreme. Instead, genuine competition is a valid force for positive change.

The independent people know that healthy and

honest competition is the motive force behind innovation. The natural world, is driven forward by this continuing innovation that occurs in response to changes in the existing environment. In the natural world, these changes are largely climactic. The life form that best adapts to these changes survives and thrives.

As an autonomous, you need to remember that competition is the lifeblood of the life progress. It not only drives innovation, but it also inspires creativity and helps build new paradigms. Don't shy away from your natural competitive nature. You are in the game to win the game, so are your fellow colleagues. Challenge yourself and challenge them in the process. Through competition, you each drive the others to better products, services, and performance. Each winner shows the way to the next level, the next round, and the next race.

Be Persistent

Ok, let's talk about persistence.

The early bird gets the worm. Slow and steady wins the race. If at first, you don't succeed, try again. If life gives you lemons make lemonade. The list goes on and on. The reason that there are so many old sayings about persistence is twofold: First, it's a really important element in success and second, it an element of success that gives a lot of people a lot of trouble. Something that's as important and troublesome as persistence deserves a lot of clichéd sayings and a lot of attention.

The problem with the road to success is that many people only picture the destination, not the journey. When they do this, they not

only fail to see that true success is not a destination (it's a lifelong process) but they also fail to see the potential problems that routinely occur when striving for success. This means that when these problems do occur, the unprepared person is stopped dead in their tracks. In their confusion, they forget where they were going and why and instead head back to where they came from.

When you are prepared for and anticipate the

setbacks that can and will happen on the journey to independent, you are ready to repair, rethink and re-engage. The persistent person understands that failure is a temporary condition that affects everyone at one time or another before they reach their goal. They also understand that failure and setback teach powerful lessons that ultimately make you stronger. As Gandhi said, strength does not come through winning. Instead, strength comes through failure. When you struggle and decide not to quit, that is the strength. It is also persistence and points up why every independent people understands that setbacks are opportunities in disguise. So don't give up.

Network and Connect

In life, you can't go it alone. Even to be independent. Bridges and boat stream traffic between all these islands and that traffic is largely information. If you cut yourself off from this flow of information, either purposely or by mistake, you do so at your own peril. Why? Because the island next to you is going to take those connections and the information they provide and use it to his or her advantage.

Networking is an essential element of every

successful one. It provides you with contacts, leads, clients, partners, suppliers and much more. It carries your name and your reputation further and more efficiently than most advertising. Most importantly, it is an endless source of profit, ideas,

collaboration, and support. If you are networking, you should do more. If you're not networking, you need to start. If you don't network, your progress in life will stagnate and die.

When you're networking you need to keep a couple of important points in mind. First, every social or professional engagement can provide you with an opportunity to network. There's often nothing more formal about it than an exchange of information and follow-up connection. Remember, as a autonomous, you're always "on the clock", so to speak. Be ready to take advantage of a potentially lucrative networking situation should the opportunity arise.

Second, when you are networking treat people naturally, the way you'd want to be treated. Offer no strings advice. Often solving a problem for free generates more long-term profit than the cost of the advice or service. Also, listen more than you talk.

Silence really can be golden when you take the time to hear what another person is saying.

Finally, always remember that honesty is the best policy. Don't promise something that you cannot produce. Don't be someone you're not in order to feel independent. Be yourself, get connected and achieve it.

Be Confident

However, true independent comes from confidence and confidence, in turn, comes from independent. They each revolve around the other in the ultimate symbiotic relationship. However, this is not a “what came first, the chicken or the egg?” kind of proposition. Confidence definitely precedes independent in the order of appearance. That’s because of the quiet assurance of true confidence, as opposed to mere cockiness, serves to lay the foundation for reaching a goal. In this way, confidence is more of an outward manifestation of an inward persona than it is a pose or an affectation. Cockiness, on the other hand, is simply an outward shield that masks an inward insecurity.

As an autonomous, you need to be confident of yourself and your abilities or skills. People react positively to a confident person, especially if that confidence is real and a part of that person's soul. In order to develop this type of true confidence, there are several things that you can do.

First, always remember that confident people are able to take a stand on an issue or a decision not because they think they are right, but because they are not afraid to be wrong. They see a difficult situation as an opportunity for growth. Finding the right solution to a problem is more important than being right. Therefore, if they are wrong they will be the first people to admit it and move on.

Confident people never afraid to admit fallibility and ask for help. They know that other people's knowledge is their greatest strength. Finally, they understand that success is a team sport. They know that any goal is achieved through the efforts of many, not the will of the few. Therefore, they share the spotlight of success and shine it on others far more than they shine it on themselves.

Do the Hustle

There's a certain urgency for been independent. This urgency doesn't apply so much to the fruits of freedom as it does to the desire for independent. You have to want to be self-standing before you can even begin to try to be. You have to want self dependent more than you want anything else. It is this desire that engenders the work ethic that's necessary to succeed. That's right, there is a definite work ethic that successful people bring to the table. If you want to succeed, then you have to emulate this work ethic. You have to want to be independent so much that you hustle.

Hustle is all about walking the success walk. Anyone can talk about success. As they say, talk is cheap. You can talk about success all day long and not get one step closer to actually being successful. The only way to reach your goals is to put in the work necessary to get these. This work requires concentration, creativity, and conscious effort. There's no secret here. You're going to have to sweat to get there. The hours are long and the tasks are consuming. There's no such thing as instant independent or overnight success. Often the people who appear to be enjoying overnight success to be independent have hustled hard for months and years to get that there. So, remember that success means work and work mean to hustle. Go the extra mile in everything you do. In the long run, those extra miles will put you ahead of the pack and that much will get you closer to self-standing

Be Passionate

There is probably nothing as important to achieving self dependent as passion. It may sound extreme, but in order to reach a goal, you have to burn for it. It has to be something that is on your mind all the time. To has to be all-consuming. In fact, passion is the flip side of our previous subject, hustle. The two go hand in hand with each other.

So, how do they work together? Well, the one requires the other. They each, in some sense, drive the other. Finally, without one, you cannot have the other. Hustling, as we discussed, is all about hard work, long hours and the extra mile. Passion is the motivation that gets all that hard work done. Face it, if you're not on fire about a project, you’re not going to be able to motivate yourself to do the hard work needed to complete that project successfully.

So, how do you obtain or maintain the passion necessary for self-dependent? Well, you should already be passionate about your hustle. If you’re not, then you need to examine why. If you’re not doing what you love to do, then you may need to think about what you are passionate about and then get into that line of work. There’s no sense and no reason to waste your time trying to be enthusiastic about something that doesn't move you. If you are already doing something you love to do, then you're halfway home. Let your love and passion for your hustle show through in that work. Your colleagues, clients and competitors will notice the difference.

Be Creative

Creativity can be elusive. It's not something that you can summon at will. When it happens, it strikes like lightning. Yet, like lightning, it can be maddeningly unpredictable. However, because creativity is an essential element of an independent mindset, it is necessary to understand the creative process and how you, looking forward to be self dependent, can cultivate your own creative juices.

The creative process is largely internal and unconscious. No one ever wakes up and says "Hey! Today I'm going to be creative." Creativity is all about taking in a lot of influences and letting those influences combines, ferment and morph in your subconscious. Together, they form a sort of

mental potting soil where new and different ideas have a chance to germinate and grow. The more things you learn, read, see and hear the more creative soil you are able to produce.

So, as a person who wants to be creative, the best thing you can do is get out there and in the world and open yourself up to new experiences. Be curious about many different things. Develop hobbies. Challenge yourself. Do the unexpected.

The more you push your own personal envelope the more you are charging your own creative batteries. When those batteries are charged, it is much more likely that inspiration will strike. Who knows where that new idea will take you?

Be Flexible

There is nothing more stifling to self dependent than rigid thinking. Rigid thinking leads to rigid behaviors and rigid behaviors lead to dead ends, blind alleys, In other words, while there is a certain amount of comfort to routine, too much routine can choke off all chances that you will be able to successfully reach your self-standing goals. Why? The answer is simple. The world is constantly changing. Rigid thinking and rigid behavior, by definition, are resistant to change. Therefore, rigidity, in thought and action, spells obsolescence in life. Everyone else moves forward while you are left behind in the dust. So what's the answer to this problem? In a word, flexibility.

In todays world, information is power, money, and control all rolled into one. The fast and free flow of information is what

makes this possible. Everything changes quickly and what is a successful formula or a popular product in one cycle can be, and usually is, old news in the next. The only way to successfully stay on top of this bucking bronco of information and use it to your advantage is to be flexible enough to roll with the changes.

Flexibility is easy to achieve as long as you are not too tied down to any single idea, skill, product, service or manner of delivery. If you keep up with changing conditions through the judicious use of the flow of information, you can easily spot new trends and adapt them successfully, usually before your competitors have had time to act. The only trick is to not fear change and, instead, embrace it. If change is the only reality in the world and change is constant in life, then, to be successful and self dependent in that world, change as to be your reality as well.

Be Positive

We've all heard a lot about the supposed power of positive thinking. We've heard how it can not only change outlooks but fortunes as well. There are probably some of you reading this right now who still remain skeptical about positivism and its alleged beneficial effects. The thing is that while healthy skepticism is fine, an entrenched and cranky skepticism is usually a sign of negative thinking. So, if you haven't tried positive thinking in your own business, yet remain skeptical of the concept, you have actually already proved that the power of positive thinking works.

Positive thinking is about enjoying the ride that life provides. It's about taking chances and seeing possibilities. It's about flexibility, creativity and developing and maintaining a strong passion for those things that you loved. It's about gusto, brio and doing things with panache. It is, in some sense, the very antithesis of rigid skepticism and preconceived negativity. It is, at its heart, an embrace of all of the powers each of us are capable of when we throw off the chains of tradition, expectation and routine results. It is a real thing and it works.

To use the power of positive thinking in your self dependent, you need to begin with a critical assessment of your own personal style and outlook. Make an honest examination of how you operate on a day to day basis. Are there areas where negativity, in any of its forms, outweighs positivity? If so, then there is room for positive change. Look at concepts like freedom, choice, possibility, optimism, and openness. Can you do more to increase your own options in any of these areas? Instead of asking yourself "How can I do this?" ask yourself instead "How can I NOT do this?"

Changing your own personal management style to one that encompasses positivity on a daily basis can give you the freedom to choose success.

Be Grateful

It is easy to expect success as if being independent was a right instead of a privilege and a gift. The problem with expecting to succeed is that, without more, the self-absorption of that expectation can slowly and subtly poison everything around you, including your self dependent. True success is earned and when it arrives it should be, and needs to be, accompanied by a strong sense of gratitude. This gratitude is not simply about being grateful for what you've achieved. It is about being grounded enough in the moment of success to remember and recognize everyone who helped you get to this particular time and place. Without this grounded gratefulness any success is lessened and will, in all likelihood, be fleeting.

So how do you repay those how helped you in achieving your goals? Well, obviously, acknowledging those individuals and sharing the benefits of your success with them is a great place to start. Yet, above and beyond taking care of your nearest and dearest, you also need to "pay it forward" by becoming a mentor and helper to others who are currently on their own journey towards success. Think about how you can collaborate with someone else in order to further their efforts. See if you can contribute in some way to their projects. This contribution doesn't have to be monetary. Advice and the wisdom of experience are often far more valuable than cold cash.

This gratitude can extend even further. There are people who are currently helping you every day that you may not see as

mentors. Look outside the box and you'll see that success and self-standing is not a solo effort, it's a team sport.

Be Accepting

There is absolutely no way for you to be successful and self-dependent until you accept who you are. You have to like yourself and what you do before anyone else will. The world detects how you feel about yourself and often simply shares the opinion you have about who you are. Be yourself and free yourself in the process. You are an individual who is unique. Your talents and abilities, your intelligence and interests, your opinions and tastes, make you who you are. There is no need to hide a part of yourself or alter a part of yourself for the sake of conformity. True success is about freedom and all truly self dependent people are individualists who have, more or less, accepted and glorified who they are. You should do the same.

At the same time, being yourself does not mean glorying in mediocrity. You need to be the very best version of yourself possible. This means that you have to work at being you. You have to put the time into self-improvement. Acceptance is not an excuse for laziness, cowardice or fear. Life is a privilege. It is a gift. The gift and the privilege of life are that you get to be yourself, the best self you can possibly be. Use the gift, take advantage of the privilege that you've been given. Don’t squander the chance. Let your own unique light shine forth. This is the light that will illuminate the path to real independent in life. It will also be the light that attracts other people to you.

Conclusion

So there you have it. Independent is a multifaceted achievement that involves many concepts and, often, many different people. However, as you've learned, the concepts involved in the successful self dependent mindset are basic and learnable principles that can easily be put into action by anyone dedicated enough to reach the next level of achievement in their lives. It is all matter of doing the work to change the things in your own personal agenda that might need adjustment. Remember that you can use this book as a tool to help you make those adjustments. You can, and should, go back and review those sections that can help you anytime the need arises. The point is that life is about success and self dependent. This means that you have your entire life to constantly change things for the better. Self dependent is a process, as well as a journey. Here's to wishing you a good trip.

Disclaimer

The writer make no representation or warranties with respect to the accuracy, applicability, fitness, and completeness of the content of this book.

The information contained in this book is strictly meant to be used for educational purposes.

If you wish to apply the ideas contained in this book, you're taking full responsibility for your actions.

www.ingramcontent.com/pod-product-compliance
Lightning Source LLC
LaVergne TN
LVHW050349160826
845677LV00014B/3869

* 9 7 9 8 8 4 6 5 1 5 4 6 8 *